Harriet Ziefert

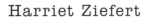

101 WAYS To Be A GOOD GRANNY

illustrations by Katie Kath

BLUE APPLE

For anyone who might be called:
Abuela, Bubbie, G-ma, Gram, Gramma, Grammie, Grams, Grandma, Granmama, Granny,
Mee Mee, Mé-Mé, Mima, Mimsy, Minny, Nana, Nonna, Oma, Ya Ya
—H.K.

To my grandmothers, women of strength and integrity, Alice Kath and Rena Dyer
—K.K.

Text copyright © 2015 by Harriet Ziefert
Illustrations copyright © 2015 by Katie Kath
All rights reserved/CIP data is available.
Published in the United States 2015 by
🍎 Blue Apple Books, 515 Valley Street,
Maplewood, NJ 07040
www.blueapplebooks.com

First Edition
Printed in China 04/15
ISBN: 978-1-60905-514-1
1 3 5 7 9 10 8 6 4 2

1. Ride bikes.

ENJOY THE
OUTDOORS

2. Go camping.

3. Grill hot dogs.

4. Catch fish.

5. Go sledding.

GUIDE A TOUR

6. Visit a factory.

7. Take a boat ride.

8. See the sights.

MAKE FROM SCRATCH

9. Cook macaroni and cheese.

10. Make soup.

11. Bake bread.

12. Cook jam.

FEED THEIR BRAINS

13. Read books.

14. Play chess.

15. Serve vegetables.

16. Play cards.

A DAY AT THE BEACH

17. Dig.

18. Build.

19. Collect.

20. Dry.

21. Supply.

TEACH

22. "I before E, except after C."

23. "Lay the shirt flat and fold the sleeves toward the center."

24. "Fork on the left.
Knife and spoon on the right."

IN THE GARDEN

25. Rake leaves.

26. Pick flowers.

27. Plant seeds.

28. Pull weeds.

29.
Water the bushes.

BE READY

30. Supply tissues.

31. Apply bandages.

32. Dab napkins.

33. Bring a clean shirt.

IN THE CAR

34. Listen to their stories.

35. Play the desired radio station.

36. Mostly say yes . . .

. . . sometimes say no.

ENTERTAIN

37.

Update your dance moves.

38.  Sing.

GIVE PRAISE

39. "Awesome!"

40.

"You're the best!"

41.

"I like that outfit."

42. "Nice hairdo!"

PLAN AN ACTIVITY

43.

Watch boats in the harbor.

44. Check out a fisherman's catch.

45. Play miniature golf.

BE PREPARED

46. Have on hand...
tape...

47. glue...

48. AA batteries...

49. markers...

50. string.

GO BACK IN IN TIME

51. Share old photos.

52. Provide vintage hats and shoes for dress-up.

53.

Sing folk songs.

WHERE HAVE all The FLOWERS GONE...

GO SHOPPING

54. Buy shoes.

55. Help choose toys.

56. Select fruit.

EXERCISE

57. Do yoga together.

58. Walk.

59. Push the swing.

MAKE ART

60. Paint.

61. Sculpt.

62. Make a collage.

TOLERATE A MESS

63. Accept mudpies . . .

64. spilled milk . . .

65. fingerpaint.

BE UP FOR ANYTHING

66. Ride the bumper cars.

START A COLLECTION

67. Gather stamps or coins . . .

68. snow globes, or glass animals . . .

69. rocks and minerals.

TRY SOMETHING NEW

70. Walk a new neighborhood.

71.
Buy lunch from a push cart.

BIG **AL'S** BIG DOGS

BE AN EXPERT

72.

"The neck of this diplodocus
is 26 feet long."

SUPPORT CHARITIES

73. Buy cookies,
or magazines,
or wrapping paper.

COMMUNICATE

74.

Have a conversation...

75. . . . or not!

BE A SPECTATOR

76. Attend a game...

77.
a school play...

78.

KEEP IN TOUCH

79.

Write letters.

80. Send cards.

BECOME A TECHIE

81. Communicate just like the kids do:
text, e-mail, or skype!

BE A GOOD SPORT

82.

Bring the birthday cake.

83. Eat the jelly beans no one else likes.

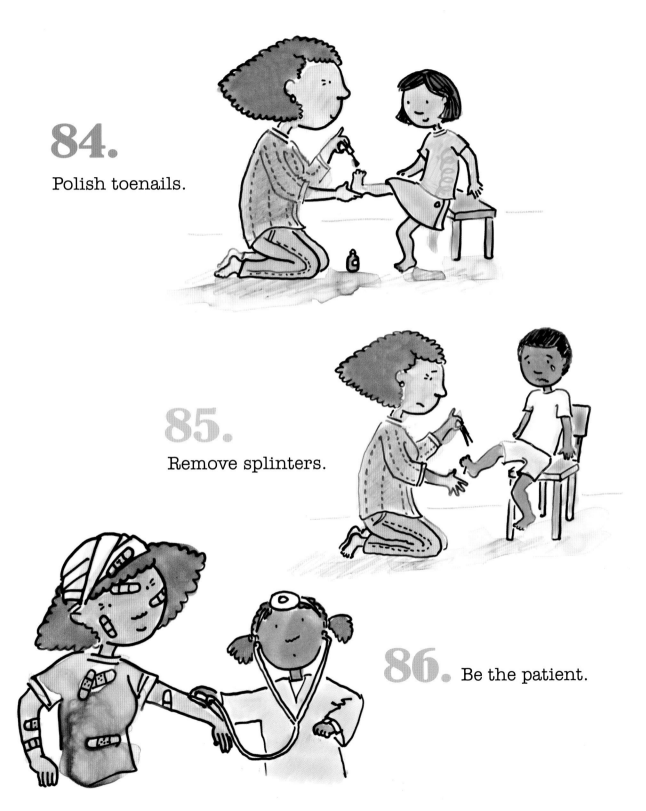

84.

Polish toenails.

85.

Remove splinters.

86. Be the patient.

BUILD

87.

Follow the instructions.*

*Don't give up even if there are more than 10 steps

88.

Assemble a dollhouse.

89.

Construct a birdhouse.

90.

Build a snow fort.

91.

Raise a tent.

LEND AN EAR

92. Listen to clarinet practice...

93. secrets...

94. reading aloud...

95. singing . . .

96. their favorite songs.

MAKE BEDTIME SPECIAL

97. Prepare a bubble bath.

98. Hold the warm towel.

99. Brush hair.

100. Serve a snack.

101. Have a sleepover!